Journey
of the
Heart
40 Days to a Transformed Life

SHEILA VANAMAN
DONNA HOPKINS SMITH

WESTBOW
PRESS®
A DIVISION OF THOMAS NELSON
& ZONDERVAN

WestBow Press books may be ordered through booksellers or by contacting:

WestBow Press
A Division of Thomas Nelson & Zondervan
1663 Liberty Drive
Bloomington, IN 47403
www.westbowpress.com
844-714-3454

ISBN: 978-1-6642-0693-9 (sc)
ISBN: 978-1-6642-0692-2 (hc)
ISBN: 978-1-6642-0694-6 (e)

Library of Congress Control Number: 2020918566

Print information available on the last page.

WestBow Press rev. date: 10/29/2020

DEDICATION

We would like to thank our husbands, John Vanaman and Tracy Smith for their love and unwavering support during the months of writing this devotion. We are thankful for their understanding of our frequent "writer retreats" so we could focus without interruption.

We would also like to acknowledge Mary Chidester and Cathy Daniels who have been our biggest cheerleaders during this project.

ACKNOWLEDGEMENT

Thank you to Mylisa Gaines, Donna Harrison, JJ and Ashley Johnson who provided us with valuable feedback on the content.

To our followers on our Facebook group, Beautifully Woven Ministries, you are our daily support and inspiration!

CONTENTS

FOREWORD

One of my favorite verses in the Bible is from the 6th Chapter of Matthew. In verse 33, Jesus says that we should "First seek His kingdom and His righteousness…" That has always been a huge part of my walk with God as well as what I teach, as a Pastor. We were created by God to be in a relationship with Him. If you don't seek Him, you are not able to fulfill your full potential as a disciple of Christ. You are not able to complete the destiny that he has designed for you. In Ephesians 2:10, Paul tells us that we are made to do good works for God, works that He prepared for us to do before we were even born. This has always been amazing to me.

Sheila and Donna have written a wonderful devotional that will help you transform your life, the life that Christ designed for you. The authors take you on a journey that is not easy, but very meaningful for you and sure to change your life. I encourage you to not just read the daily devotion, but to meditate on each one, go thru the Scriptures and let the Holy Spirit touch your heart and spirit. Draw near to God and He will draw near to you. James 4:8

Rev. Jim Stilwell
Christ United Methodist Church
Tulsa, OK

INTRODUCTION

Psalm 139:13-16 (NIV) says For you created my inmost being; [13] you knit me together in my mother's womb.[14] I praise you because I am fearfully and wonderfully made; your works are wonderful, I know that full well. [15] My frame was not hidden from you when I was made in the secret place, when I was woven together in the depths of the earth.[16] Your eyes saw my unformed body; all the days ordained for me were written in your book before one of them came to be.

Beautifully Woven Ministries used this passage of scripture as our framework when choosing our ministry name. We want God's people to know they are valued and loved by our Father.

There are so many events occurring in our world that affect our stress level. Racism, politics, unstable stock market, disease, natural disasters all affect our emotions. Added to this stress, there are many issues that affect us. Because of past mistakes, some think they may not be worthy of God's love and think God could not possibly use us.

The very God of the universe cared enough to knit us together, He created us in his image, He knows us intimately. First, God needs us to know our value. Until we can grasp the concept that we are

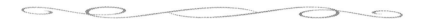

valued, we cannot release our cares and truly trust that He will guide our life and has everything under control.

We have created this devotional to be a journey of the heart. We have included four important steps. The four areas include Calming the Storm, Attitude of Prayer, Surrendering to God's Will, and The Road to a Transformed Life. We have provided a devotional, a page to journal, and an accompanying study guide in this book. As you take this journey, we hope you will learn to be still and listen to God's voice.

Day 1

He says, "Be still, and know that I am God; I will be exalted among the nations, I will be exalted in the earth." Psalm 46:10 (NIV)

We must understand this Psalm was written during a time of strife and war. God was directing His people to stand firm and open their eyes to who He is. Some interpret this as He was instructing them to stop fighting, because He had conquered the enemy.

This scripture is a message I receive from God often. I find myself worrying about things I cannot control. Frequently I am my own worst enemy, then God gently whispers, "Relax my child, Be Still, I've got this. "He wants me to understand He is a sovereign God, and above all else, He will fight my battles.

Our anxious thoughts may not be because of war, such as when the Psalm was written, but nonetheless, they are real. If we allow these thoughts to dictate our actions, we may find ourselves in a place of hopelessness. When we are apprehensive regarding a situation in our life, it often feels as though we are at war. Regardless of the circumstance, God wants us to allow Him to fight for us.

It is not easy to stay calm when we are amidst a storm. God still wants us to understand that worry and frustration does not solve the problem; it only hinders progress. Many times, we need to stop, take a breath, and release it to God. In that moment, we must quiet our mind and meditate on scripture. We must rest in confidence that above all else, He is God. As we rest in this confidence, we become more intimate with our Lord and can live our lives with the assurance that He is the shelter within our storm. Our only job is to Be Still and KNOW...

Prayer

Father, I believe that you do not want us to strive and be anxious about anything. I know nothing is too big that you cannot handle. You see every situation, and you hold my future in your hands. Lord, teach me to be still. In Jesus' name, Amen!

Read Psalm 46 and meditate on this passage of scripture.

Journal what God showed you during your time of meditation.

Day 2

He got up, rebuked the wind and said to the waves, "Quiet! Be still!" Then the wind died down and it was completely calm. He said to his disciples, "Why are you so afraid? Do you still have no faith?" They were terrified and asked each other, "Who is this? Even the wind and the waves obey him!" Mark 4:39-41

Jesus's example of remaining calm proved to the disciples that He did not fear the storm; in fact, He was sleeping peacefully while the storm raged. The lesson the disciples learned was they must lean on Jesus and trust that He could rebuke the wind. In this passage, Jesus proved that He had authority over all creation. The disciples found themselves in awe of Jesus that even the wind and the sea obeyed Him.

At times of trouble, we must pause and think about what is essential in life. We should reevaluate our own lives and take note of what matters most. Is it our family, friendships, or peace with our maker? For example, when my son passed away, it rocked my world, just as the boat was rocking in the storm. Regardless of the situation or the storm that rages in our life, the anxious thought can consume us. If we allow emotions to dictate our feelings, they can take root in the depths of our soul. We must turn our eyes to Jesus when we are troubled; only He can calm the storm that rages within.

Prayer

Father, you know the storm, that is raging in my life, and you know my fears. I pray that you take all my anxious thoughts captive, just like you calmed the storm for your disciple. I know you are in control

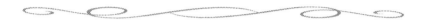

of my situation. May I come through this a better person. I know you, and only you hold my future. In Jesus' name, I pray, Amen!

Read Luke 8:25 – 27 and Matthew 8: 23 – 27 for their accounts of Jesus calming the storm.

Meditate on these scriptures and allow Him to calm your storm. Journal your thoughts after reading different accounts.

Day 3

This is why I remind you to fan into flames the spiritual gift God gave you when I laid my hands on you. ⁷For God has not given us a spirit of fear and timidity, but of power, love, and self-discipline. 2 Timothy 1:6-7 (NLT)

The King James version uses the term "sound mind" instead of self-control and this is found only in 2 Timothy 1:7. The original Greek word is *sophronismos*, which some interpret as self-control or self-discipline. In other words, a mind that is controlled by the Spirit, not my humanness.

Paul wrote this deeply personal letter to Timothy, appealing to him to not lose faith, even if he came under attack. He knew his time of death was near, and Timothy would need strength to carry on. Paul knew Timothy was naturally timid, which is what scripture is referring to when it states a spirit of fear. Paul wanted Timothy to draw on the strength and power which was instilled in him through Christ. Timothy needed to realize the Holy Spirit would provide the passion and courage needed to carry on.

God's desire for us to not lose faith when we are faced with adversity. At times it feels as if we are being attacked from every direction. Instead of giving in to fear, we must lay our burdens at the foot of the cross. Our deep bond with our Savior will see us through trials if we only lean into him. We must cling to our faith and abide in Christ. His Spirit lives in us, and we must hold fast to our faith because fear is the opposite of faith. If we truly have faith, we must lay it at His feet, and not listen to the voices of doubt in our head. God's Spirit gives us the power to overcome the enemy. His Spirit is like an immovable anchor that we cling to. Therefore, we must focus

our mind on Christ instead of ourselves or our situation, because in Him we have infinite power and strength.

Prayer

Father, deliver me from my fear. Fill me with your Holy Spirit, so I may gain strength to overcome the enemy. I desire to increase my faith in you. Help me not to listen to the voices in my head. In Jesus' name, I pray Amen.

Read 2 Timothy 1:6-11

Meditate on this passage of scripture. Journal your thoughts of what it means to have a sound mind.

Day 4

Moses answered the people, "Do not be afraid. Stand firm and you will see the deliverance the LORD will bring you today. The Egyptians you see today you will never see again. The LORD will fight for you; you need only to be still." Exodus 14:13-14

In this passage of scripture, the Israelites were surrounded by Pharaoh's army. They were trapped and had to either fight or surrender. They feared for their life and begged Moses to allow them to quit, even though it meant going back to being slaves. They had lost hope and did not trust that God would defend them. Moses appealed to them to stand firm and have faith they would be delivered. Moses stretched out his staff as instructed by God; the Red Sea parted so the Israelites could go through. After they reached the other side, the sea flowed back and drowned Pharaoh's army. God had a plan to deliver them as promised, they needed to be still and trust that He would fight for them.

We can relate to the Israelites since we fret and worry when faced with the unknown. We prefer to turn back because we do not want to leave our comfort zone, even when we are not in a good situation. God wants us to trust Him, and He will make a way through the struggle. The example of the Israelites is a crucial reminder, the Lord will fight our battles too, if we only stand firm on His word. We must develop a pattern of depending on God, so after we come through the struggle, we will see He was in control all along, even when we could not see it. We must believe God will show up for us in a miraculous way, just as He did for the Israelites!

Prayer

Father, help me to be still long enough to see you are Lord, and you will see me through. Help me to trust that what you have for my future is far better than anything I could imagine. I believe that you are fighting for me. Amen.

Read Exodus 14

Meditate on this passage of scripture. Journal how you will allow God to fight for you.

Day 5

So do not fear, for I am with you; do not be dismayed, for I am your God.

I will strengthen you and help you; I will uphold you with my righteous right hand. Isaiah 41:10

God wants the Israelites to understand they are His chosen people, descendants of Abraham. He is assuring them that even though danger looms, He will protect them, and they will be delivered. God needed them to know that He would provide the strength they required and did not want His people to be disappointed in the bleak circumstances.

God does not wish for us to live in a spirit of fear any more than He wanted the Israelites to be afraid. The very God of the universe is telling us He is with us and does not want us to live in despair. God is fully aware that doubt and discouragement can be triggered by past experiences, and He wants us to know He is with us and will not forsake us. He gives us the strength to conquer the doubt and anxiety that rules our minds. When we apply his word in our lives, we realize we can overcome our fear and quiet the chattering monkeys in our heads. We are chosen by God, and He gives us the strength to maneuver any obstacles in our way. In times of trouble, we need to lean on our Father, draw from His power, and prevail over the enemy. Even better, He will empower us, His children, and only He will sustain us. So, draw from His strength, allow Him to silence your fears, and believe He is God, and He can! Remember this verse from Philippians 4:13, "I can do all things through Christ who strengthens me."

Prayer

Father, I do not want to walk in fear. Please calm the voices in my head so I may plant Your Word in my heart. Amen.

Read Isaiah 41 8-13.

Meditate on this passage of scripture. Journal about a time you had to trust God. Did you pray for strength?

Day 6

Do not be anxious about anything, but in every situation, by prayer and petition, with thanksgiving, present your requests to God. [7]And the peace of God, which transcends all understanding, will guard your hearts and your minds in Christ Jesus. Philippians 4:6-7

I am amazed when I think about Paul's transformation, the depth of his love for Christ, and his unwavering faith. Despite being imprisoned, Paul is joyful when he writes this letter to the Philippians. Unlike letters to other churches, Paul is complimentary of the faith and obedience the Philippians have shown. Paul understands they still have much to learn and is clearly addressing their need to grow in Christ. He encourages them to take everything to Christ in prayer and petition. His desire is for them to find the peace that transcends all understanding.

Like the Philippians, Christ aspires us to bring everything to Him in prayer, He will meet our needs. We must recognize Christ has the power to intervene in all circumstances, good and bad. This means laying all our cares at the altar, not just the burdens, but also the good things. We must submit our will, and He will give us a peace that will surpass our comprehension. Think about it; in our chaotic multi-tasking lives, we cannot conceive that kind of order on our own, which is a peace that only He can offer us. We should all desire to have the kind of peace that Paul had, regardless of our circumstance. When we achieve this kind of peace, the Holy Spirit will comfort us and overpower all our sorrow.

Prayer

Father, give me the kind of peace that will go beyond my humanness. Help me to slow down amidst the chaos and fill me with your Spirit that I may rest in your love. In Jesus' name, I pray Amen.

Read Philippians 4: 4-9

Meditate on this passage of scripture. Journal what God showed you during your time of meditation regarding relinquishing control of your heart and mind to him.

Day 7

Are not two sparrows sold for a penny? Yet not one of them will fall to the ground outside your Father's care.[a] 30 And even the very hairs of your head are all numbered. 31 So do not be afraid; you are worth more than many sparrows. Matthew 10:29-31

The reference of the sparrow was to demonstrate to the disciples how valued they are in God's eyes. When Jesus chose the disciples, they were ordinary everyday men from all walks of life. Jesus was preparing His disciples for a future ministry, spreading the gospel. He wanted them to understand there would be persecution and hard times, but He also needed them to realize their value. Jesus desired them to stand firm in their faith and have the courage to press on after His crucifixion and resurrection. The disciples were explicitly chosen to carry the gospel throughout the known world. Their ministry was the foundation of the Christian life we know today.

Think about the fact that every hair on our head is numbered. Perhaps you are concerned with a situation that you feel God would not necessarily see as important. As the psalmist says, "he knit me together in my mother's womb. I am fearfully and wonderfully made" This validates how great His love is for us and how much He cares. It is unfathomable to imagine a love so deep as the love God has for His children. His desire is for us to be in harmony with Him, for we were designed for a deep-rooted relationship with Christ. He created us in His image, and we are treasured beyond comprehension.

Prayer

Father, I want to put all my trust in you that I may love others the way you love me. I want to know you in such a way that I commit myself totally to you. Help me to thank you for the small things in my life. In Jesus' name, I pray Amen.

Read Luke 12:7 and Matthew 10: 29-31 for their accounts of the passage of scripture.

Meditate on these passages of scripture. Journal how you feel about God's love for you.

Day 8

I will bless the LORD at all times; his praise shall continually be in my mouth. My soul makes its boast in the LORD; let the humble hear and be glad. Oh, magnify the LORD with me, and let us exalt his name together! I sought the LORD, and he answered me and delivered me from all my fears. Psalm 34:1-4 (ESV)

David understood that he was imperfect, but nonetheless, he had a desire to be whole. He realized he must bow before the Lord in an attitude of prayer. David had faith that God would hear his cry and deliver him from evil. And how marvelous he was to appreciate that he must give God the glory for every victory and go to Him with every need. 1 Samuel 13:14 (paraphrased) says David was a man after God's own heart; perhaps that was because he fervently poured out his heart to God, or maybe it is his character traits such as humbleness and a sincere devotion to God.

Perhaps in our weakness, we can learn from David, the art of taking every decision and laying every sin to the Lord. May we learn how to sing His praise in all things. We must understand we are imperfect but can be made whole through a consecrated life in Christ.

Sometimes we find ourselves grumbling and worrying when we are going through a trial, instead of praising Him in the storm. May we learn that God will answer our prayers and free us from the bonds of apprehension. We do not have to live our lives in a spirit of fear. We can be set free from the chains of the enemy if we place our trust in God. We should shout our praise from the mountain top.

Prayer

Father, please loose the chains of fear that bind me. Help me to trust in you rather than worry. I know you will see me through my iniquities. In Jesus' name, I pray Amen.

Read Psalm 34:1-4 Meditate on this passage of scripture. Journal your thoughts about praising God when you do not have answers.

Day 9

Do you not know? Have you not heard? The LORD is the everlasting God, the Creator of the ends of the earth. He will not grow tired or weary, and his understanding no one can fathom.

He gives strength to the weary and increases the power of the weak. Even youths grow tired and weary, and young men stumble and fall; but those who hope in the LORD will renew their strength. They will soar on wings like eagles; they will run and not grow weary; they will walk and not be faint. Isaiah 40:28-31

In this passage of scripture, we learn God's people had grown weary. God wanted them to understand that He does not become weary. They had been defeated, and quite frankly, they were exhausted. They knew He had promised to bring them back to Jerusalem; however, they were growing tired of waiting. God needed them to understand that if they trusted Him, he would renew their strength, refresh their souls, so they could soar.

Some schools of thought say an eagle portrays the power and strength of the Spirit working in our lives. It is said an eagle's grip is ten times the strength of a human handshake. Eagles are strong, often fly alone, and soar high above the clouds.

When we find ourselves amid chaos, we often feel alone and hopeless. We are tired, broken, and at the brink of giving up. We are desperate for answers and feel God has abandoned us. We lose faith in ourselves and God. At times like this, it is crucial to bring ourselves to a place of rest, so He can provide us strength. God does not grow weary, nor does He forsake his children, but God's timing is not our timing. We must learn to wait upon the Lord, trust even

when we do not feel His presence. He will show up in His time in a mighty way! He will provide us the strength we need to soar with the eagles.

Prayer

Father, help me to meditate on you, quiet my mind so I may rest in you. Refresh my soul, so I can fly with the eagles. In Jesus' name, I pray Amen.

Read Isaiah 40:28-31 Meditate on this passage of scripture. Do you find it difficult to wait on God? Journal about your difficulty with waiting for his timing.

Day 10

But blessed is the one who trusts in the LORD, whose confidence is in him. They will be like a tree planted by the water that sends out its roots by the stream. It does not fear when heat comes; its leaves are always green. It has no worries in a year of drought and never fails to bear fruit. Jeremiah 17:7-8

Jeremiah was a man of steadfast faith who placed all his trust in God and was deeply rooted in His belief. Many reference Jeremiah as the weeping prophet because he deeply desired the people to be rooted in God rather than idols. Even after hearing Jeremiah's message of sin, Judah did not respond and continued to worship idols. Even though Jeremiah's life was marked by great suffering and imprisonment, his faith never faltered. God saw that Jeremiah was faithful and delivered him.

Water mostly enters a tree through the roots by osmosis, and any dissolved mineral nutrients will travel upward through the inner bark's xylem (using capillary action) and into the leaves. These traveling nutrients then feed the tree through the process of leaf photosynthesis.[1]

We should desire to achieve the faith like Jeremiah, regardless what happens, we will not waiver in our faith. The scripture serves as a reminder that as Christians, we must be like the tree planted by the water, and just as a tree needs essential nutrients to produce green leaves and fresh fruit, we need to absorb the word of God to flourish. A tree that is planted by the water never thirsts, because the water is plentiful. If we are deeply rooted in God, when trouble arises, we will have the strength to withstand the storm.

Prayer

Father, I realize I need to thirst for more of you, I want to be deeply rooted in your word. Grant in me the desire to flourish and be a Jeremiah for you. In Jesus' name, I pray Amen.

Read Jeremiah 17:7-8 Meditate on this passage of scripture. Journal about what God showed you during your time of meditation.

Day 11

I urge, then, first of all, that petitions, prayers, intercession and thanksgiving be made for all people, for kings and all those in authority, that we may live peaceful and quiet lives in all godliness and holiness. This is good, and pleases God our Savior, who wants all people to be saved and to come to a knowledge of the truth. 1 Timothy 2:1-4

The elements of sincere prayer are adoration, confession, supplication, intercession and thanksgiving. [2]

Supplication (also known as petitioning) is a form of prayer, wherein one party humbly or earnestly asks another party to provide something, either for the party who is doing the supplicating (e.g., "Please spare my life.") or on behalf of someone else. [3]

We petition God daily. Many of our petitions are simple: safe travels, safety of our kids, or maybe we are praying just to have a good day.

Don't you think God wants to answer those big prayers, like the Joshua sun stand still kind of a prayer? How about Daniel in the lion's den prayer, or maybe even a Jericho wall coming down prayer? He wants to show us his power and glory! Why not believe Him for something big? Pray for something you cannot accomplish on your own! Steven Furtick, pastor of Elevation Church in Charlotte, NC calls this kind of prayer an audacious prayer. IF we believe that God is bigger than life, we need to believe He can answer an audacious prayer! What better way for God to get the glory than to pray for something only He can accomplish! Michael Todd, pastor of Transformation Church in Tulsa, OK was believing the church would purchase the Spirit Bank Event Center, and it was not for sale

at that time. In the end, the church purchased the center and are holding services there. Read their encouraging stories so that you may be able to plant your seed of faith in something big!

Prayer

Father, I thank you for the blessings that you have given to me. Help me to believe in your power and to be bold in my prayers so that I may glorify you in all that I say and do. Help me to witness to others so that they may see you thru me.

Read the verses listed in elements of prayer and meditate on the words of the scripture. Journal your thoughts regarding the various elements and types of prayer. Do you have a favorite?

Day 12

And pray in the Spirit on all occasions with all kinds of prayers and requests. With this in mind, be alert and always keep on praying for all the Lord's people. Ephesians 6:18

We are instructed by this verse to pray and to bring our requests to our heavenly Father. He provided us an example of a prayer to guide us in bringing those requests to him. The Lord's prayer is found in two of the gospels, Matthew chapter 6 and Luke chapter 11. The Lord's prayer is probably the most widely known prayer amongst Christians:

"Our Father who art in heaven, hallowed be thy name.
Thy kingdom come. Thy will be done on earth as it is in
heaven. Give us this day our daily bread, and forgive us our
trespasses, as we forgive those who trespass against us, and
lead us not into temptation, but deliver us from evil.
For thine is the kingdom and the power, and
the glory, forever and ever. Amen"

By praying this perfect prayer, we are acknowledging our Father for who He is, and worshipping Him with praise and adoration. We are relinquishing our control and giving it back to the one who is in control and petitioning Him with our desires. Confession is another important piece of this prayer. We close our prayer by asking for protection in this world of sin.

As we pray this perfect prayer, remember it is not just something to be memorized and repeated every day, God wants us to have an intimate relationship with Him, and desires to hear our heart.

I encourage you to find a quiet place to be alone with God and begin reading scriptures about prayer. Find your own love language to God. He already knows your heart but wants you to share it with Him.

Call unto me, and I will answer thee, and show thee great and mighty things, which thou knowest not. Jeremiah 33:3

Prayer

Father, we come to you today to thank you for who you are and what you mean to me in my life. You are the alpha and omega, the beginning, and the end. Help us Father as we trudge thru live, make us aware of our sins so that we can confess them to you and learn life's lessons your way. We pray for your guidance and protection as we go throughout the day. Amen

Focus on the Lord's prayer during your quiet time and journal its meaning to you.

Day 13

Rejoice always, pray continually, give thanks in all circumstances; for this is God's will for you in Christ Jesus. I Thessalonians 5:16-18

Prayer is not just about speaking beautiful eloquent words or spending a certain amount of time in prayer each day. The Bible tells us to pray without ceasing. It is important to have a quiet time with the Lord each day, so we can communicate our needs and listen for His instructions. This conversation can continue throughout the day.

I know when I find a spot that is close to the front door of the grocery store, I always rejoice and thank Him and claim "Blessed and Highly favored". Some people may think I am crazy, but it is in the little things that we please Him. We can find God in nature, flowers, trees and butterflies. We must slow down in our fast-paced lives and recognize that he is omnipresent.

The quickest way to get over a "mood' is to start praying and praising the Father. Christian singer-songwriter Matt Maher has a current song, "Alive and Breathing", the chorus of the song reflects what I am saying:

> Joy still comes in the morning
> Hope still walks with the hurting
> If you're still alive and breathing
> Praise the Lord

Do not stress about formatting your perfect prayer, just begin speaking to the Father like He is your best friend. Believe me, He can handle anything we have to say.

Prayer

Our gracious Father, we come to you today thanking you for your blessings and giving us the gift of life for another day. Help us to become more like you, forgiving others even if we feel that they do not deserve it. Change our vision so that we see people thru your lens, loving all your creation in a way that only you can. Amen

Read 1 Thessalonians Chapter 5 and journal your thoughts. What is Paul telling us?

Day 14

In the same way, the Spirit helps us in our weakness. We do not know what we ought to pray for, but the Spirit himself intercedes for us through wordless groans. Romans 8:26 NIV

Have you ever been in the middle of something and all you could do is cry? You cannot even pull yourself together to pray? Some might even say you are a "hot mess". Scripture tells us the Holy Spirit will intercede for us.

According to The Free Dictionary the meaning of intercedes is *to plead on another's behalf.*

In the Old Testament, Abraham interceded with the Lord for the righteous of Sodom to be spared. During Jesus' final days on this earth, He prepares His disciples for his death and for the days to come without him. In John 16:7, He speaks to them: Nevertheless I tell you the truth; it is expedient for you that I go away: for if I go not away, the Comforter will not come unto you; but if I depart, I will send him unto you.

If He cared for His disciples enough to prepare them and leave them with an intercessor; don't you think He cares the same for you? The Bible also tells us in Romans, chapter 8 that NOTHING can separate us from the love of God! Do you feel unworthy, not smart enough, not pretty enough? Maybe you have a past, but don't we all?

The scripture reminds us: For I am persuaded that neither death, nor life, nor angels, nor principalities, nor powers, nor things present, nor things to come. Nor height, nor depth, nor any other creature,

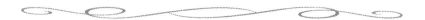

shall be able to separate us from the love of God, which is in Christ Jesus our Lord. Romans 8: 38-39

Prayer

Father, we are thankful for the Holy Spirit who intercedes on our behalf. Help us to focus daily on our walk with you, strengthening our dependence on you and learning to hear your voice. Amen

Read John chapter 16 and journal your thoughts of what Jesus is telling the disciples.

Day 15

Jabez was more honorable than his brothers. His mother had named him Jabez,[a] saying, "I gave birth to him in pain." [10] Jabez cried out to the God of Israel, "Oh, that you would bless me and enlarge my territory! Let your hand be with me, and keep me from harm so that I will be free from pain." And God granted his request. I Chronicles 4: 9-10 (NIV)

As Jabez prayed to God, our Father, do you think he had doubts? What do you think "increased territory" meant? I have this prayer many times over the years, and even completed *The Prayer of Jabez* study by Bruce Wilkinson with my close friend and co-author and what I can tell you, IT IS LIFE CHANGING!

By praying the Jabez prayer, we are asking God for more. Yes, you read that correctly, we are asking for it! God has so much for us. In Ephesians chapter 3, Paul is encouraging the believers to walk as fruitful followers of Christ and to serve in unity and love in the midst of persecution. Verse 20 reads, "Now unto him that is able to do exceedingly abundantly above all that we ask or think, according to the power that worketh in us.".

God wants to answer our prayers, He is our Father, and what Father does not want to help His child? Go into this prayer with an open heart; He will speak to you and will show you the territory He has reserved just for you. Many times, our territory lies within our God-given talents and interests. Remember, He promised it will be exceedingly abundantly more than we can ask or imagine!

Prayer

Heavenly Father, we praise you for who you are! Guide and direct our steps on this journey of life and show us the specific territory you have outlined for our paths. Your word promises us that you will be our guide, and comforter through it all. Help us to quiet our minds and hear your direction. Give us peace as we travel through the unknown. Amen

During your quiet time, journal what your "Jabez prayer" might sound like. What are your deepest desires?

Day 16

Very early in the morning, while it was still dark, Jesus got up, left the house and went off to a solitary place, where he prayed. Mark 1:35

We should make our prayer time a priority and give our full attention to the Lord. You may have to get creative to have that alone time, and you must be willing to sacrifice. Maybe you sacrifice a little sleep and get up early, maybe you sacrifice time with friends or entertainment, so that you can guarantee that quality time in prayer.

Moses and Jesus have similar experiences recorded in the Bible. Both men had not only wilderness experiences, but they also had a mountain top experience. God uses wilderness experiences in our lives as a place where we feel isolated so that He has our full attention.

Sometimes we may need to isolate ourselves in a quiet place, retreat from everyone to gain clarity on a situation or tune into the voice of God without interruption. Some people have a designated quiet spot or certain time they pray where they can be without interruption. In the movie, *The War Room*, Miss Clara has a prayer closet where she can go to shout out her bold prayers. Jesus was known to go to the mountain to isolate and pray, and before His death, Jesus went to the Garden of Gethsemane on the Mount of Olives to pray.

Are you feeling isolated by circumstances in your life? Go to the one who will listen without judgement, respond with love, and calm your spirit. Make it a priority to get quiet before God, He wants to hear your heart.

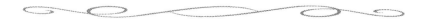

Prayer

Father, humble me today so that I can hear Your voice. Help me to block out all the distractions of this world so that I can focus totally and completely on you. Amen

Write in your journal your feelings about your life right now, get quiet before God and tell him the desires of your heart.

Day 17

Now faith is the substance of things hoped for the evidence of things not seen. Hebrews 11:1. (KJV)

Are you praying for something big in your life? Do you believe that it will be answered? How is your faith meter? The Word tells us that we just need faith the size of a mustard seed, which is about the size of a bb pellet. When you plant the seed, it grows into a mustard bush and will reach an average mature height of between 6 and 20 feet with a 20-foot spread, and under ideal conditions, a plant may grow to 30 feet tall.

What type of faith seeds are you planting? Are you watering your faith routinely with prayer and fertilizing with devotion? Joshua had faith when he asked the Lord to have the sun remain in the sky so he could defeat his enemies. The Samaritan woman believed she could be healed, if she could touch the hem of Jesus' garment. Shadrach, Meschach and Abednego had faith when they were thrown into the fiery furnace.

Just because something happened in Biblical times, does not mean prayers and miracles are not happening today. I can recall a couple of miracles that I have personally been a part of. Our pastor's newborn grandson, Gabriel had failed several hearing tests after birth. His parents were concerned about an unknown future of raising a hearing-impaired child. God had other plans. His grandfather, our pastor, had a prayer time at the end of the service and the baby was brought to the front, where he was anointed with oil and the saints prayed a prayer of healing for that child. Within a few days, he was responding to voices and noises in the home, and on a follow up appointment passed his hearing test with flying colors.

My daughter is another example of a miracle. In her late 20's she was diagnosed with epilepsy. In her early thirties, she was driving on a four-lane road in a busy town and had a seizure and blacked out. She ran through several major intersections, going the wrong way and running through several red lights! The highway patrol saw her and not knowing the situation, followed her in pursuit. As she came to a railroad crossing, her car veered toward the center line and ran upon the concrete embankment, halting the car. She came out of it with bruises from her seat belt, but nothing else. The damage to the car involved the undercarriage, nothing visible. Later that afternoon when we went to the salvage to view her car, the owner asked how the driver was doing, not knowing the girl with us was our daughter. He said to her, "Someone else was driving this car for you young lady"!

Prayer

Father, forgive me and my lack of faith. Help me to trust you in all areas of my life, and to be thankful for all answers to prayer no matter the size. Amen

What miracles have you seen or known about in your life? Write about them in your journal today. Are you believing for a miracle in your life today? Write it in your journal and claim God's power by faith.

Day 18

Say to this mountain, "Move from here to there," and it will move."
Matthew 17:20 (KJV)

Having faith in the spoken word is another key factor in prayer. Speak life to your dreams, ambitions and prayers. In Genesis, God said "let there be light, and there was light". The power of the spoken word is seen many more times during the creation of the heavens and the earth.

Do you see the process? Pray, have faith and speak God's word. Keep this Book of the Law always on your lips; meditate on it day and night, so that you may be careful to do everything written in it. Then you will be prosperous and successful. Joshua 1:8

We can allow negative self-talk to ruin us as an individual, causing anxiety and depression, or we can speak God's word over ourselves, and rise above. The same thing for our prayer life, it is essential that we expect great things to happen.

My God will do exceedingly abundantly more than we can ask or imagine.

My God will supply all your needs according to his riches and glory,

Call upon me, and I will answer you, and show you great and mighty things that you do not know.

If you are a mature Christian, you could list hundreds of scriptures that reveal God's promises to us. If you are a baby Christian, welcome aboard, God has some great things in store for you. Even through

trials, God's word stands strong. He has promised He will never leave us nor forsake us.

Prayer

Father, thank you for your word that is guiding and directing our lives. Bring to my attention anything that I speak that is negative about my life. I know that tests build my faith, help me to stand firm on your word. Thank you for everything you have done and are doing in my life. Amen

For your journal activity today, think about your negative self- talk and list those so that you can focus on the positive. Turn the negative statement into a positive one.

Day 19

For as the body without the spirit is dead, so faith without works is dead also. James 2:26 (KJV)

Now that you have petitioned God with your desires, you have a job to do. Many times, our prayers require us to take action. If you are praying for a job, then start applying, dress your best for the interview and speak positive words over your situation. You cannot sit on the sidelines as a spectator, you must take an active role to fuel your faith.

Esther is a biblical example of a woman who acted. King Xerxes admired Esther and made her Queen, not knowing she was of Jewish descent. Esther's uncle Mordecai found out about a plot to kill the Jewish people, and he plead with Esther to do something about it. Esther went against the palace protocol and approached the King, without being summoned. She begged for her people to be spared; her action saving the lives of her people. Had she been fearful or hesitant to go against the royal protocol, the people would have been destroyed.

Maybe you have been praying for something, and you need to act upon it. Bring your petition to the Lord, listen to His voice and act and do your part. Who knows, perhaps you were made for such a time as this. Paraphrased Esther 4:14

Prayer

Father, help me to be more like Esther. Help me to see the need and quickly respond. Help me to develop a proactive response in my

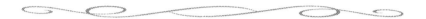

prayer life, to be an active participant. Thank you for molding me and preparing me for more. Amen

As you journal today, is the Lord telling you something that you need to do? What is holding you back? List the reasons you have not followed through with the task and pray to overcome the barriers.

Day 20

Blessed are those who hear the word of God and obey it. Luke 11:28 (KJV)

Today is our tenth day of focusing on prayer and learning to hear God's voice in our lives. But we must do more than hear His voice, we must respond and obey. Think about this: what if the soldiers had stopped marching around Jericho on day 6? What if Jonah had refused the Nineveh assignment? Would he have stayed in the belly of the whale? What if Noah chose not to build the ark? Would we even be here today? What if Esther refused to talk to the King? Would the Jewish people have been slaughtered?

We are the one missing out on a blessing because we are not following through on our God-given assignment. We need to stop being so selfish and self-serving and focus on others. Maybe our assignment is not about you at all? Maybe you are just the conduit to reach someone else? I have always thought about my various jobs as an assignment from God. Jobs are the means to reach and influence people for the kingdom. Your assignment is not about your pay rate, your job title or location on the corporate ladder. It is about the kingdom! A bigger title equals more influence for God. How are you acting in your position? Are you the reflection of God? Are you a tyrannical leader? If so, you might want to start reading this book from the beginning and start over.

If God has instructed you to do a task, start a ministry, write or book or whatever the assignment, your goal should be to get it accomplished. "But seek first his kingdom and his righteousness, and all these things will be given to you as well.". Matthew 6:33

Prayer

Father, thank you for your blessings in my life. Guide and direct me in the paths that you would have for me, so that I may glorify you. Forgive me where I have failed you, show me your ways. Amen

Continue journaling about your barriers from yesterday and write scripture beside each barrier that says you CAN!

Day 21

Then he reached out his hand and took the knife to slay his son. ¹¹But the angel of the LORD called out to him from heaven, "Abraham! Abraham! "Here I am," he replied, "Do not lay a hand on the boy," he said. "Do not do anything to him. Now I know that you fear God, because you have not withheld from me your son, your only son." Genesis 22:10-12

I cannot think of a more beautiful example of a life surrendered to God than Abraham's. When God instructed Abraham to take his son to Moriah and offer him as a burnt offering, Abraham obeyed and did not question God. The NIV states in Genesis 22:5 NIV, "Stay here with the donkey while I and the boy go over there. We will worship and then we will come back to you." This statement demonstrates Abraham's steadfast faith that God would provide a sacrifice. Nonetheless, he complied with God's instruction, with the knife in hand he was ready to slay his son. The angel of the Lord intervened, and God provided a sacrifice. God spared Isaac's life because of his Father's obedience.

Abraham's story symbolizes the sacrifice God made for us when He sent his son to die for our sins. It speaks of the depth of God's love for His children. Could we make the ultimate sacrifice and not sway in our faith in God? Strong faith leads to a life of obedience.

We, too, must relinquish our life to God's will. Obedience is not easy; it requires sacrifice and perseverance. To live in obedience will ultimately bring a beautiful life.

Prayer

Father, I want to live a life fully surrendered to you. Instill in me a deep desire to say not my will, but thy will be done. Amen.

Read Genesis 22

Meditate on this passage of scripture. How would you feel if you were asked to make the same sacrifice as Abraham? Journal your thoughts.

Day 22

"Go," the LORD said to me, "and lead the people on their way, so that they may enter and possess the land I swore to their ancestors to give them." And now, Israel, what does the LORD your God ask of you but to fear the LORD your God, to walk in obedience to him, to love him, to serve the LORD your God with all your heart and with all your soul. Deuteronomy 10: 11-12 (NIV)

God was fulfilling His promise to the Israelites. After wandering in the desert for forty years, it was time for this new generation of Israelites to enter Canaan, the land of milk and honey. Because of their disbelief, Moses had to intercede on their behalf, and God accepted Moses as the intercessor. Because of their distrust, Moses reminded the Israelites that God was showing them mercy. This was Moses's final instruction before transferring leadership to Joshua, who would lead them into the Canaan land.

What does God ask of us? He asks us to fear the Lord, to hold His name above all other names. We are to walk in obedience and submit to His will. We must live a life surrendered to His will and love Him with our heart, soul, and mind. To genuinely love God with all our being may sound easy, but in reality, this requires sacrifice. We must surrender daily, sacrificing our desires if we want to drift toward Godliness. We must come to a place where we can say Lord, I am willing to do whatever you require. A journey of the heart involves obedience that will ultimately lead to a blessed life.

Prayer

Father, I submit my will to you. I desire to know you intimately so that I may love you with all my heart, soul, and mind. Amen

Read Deuteronomy 10:10-12

Meditate on this passage of scripture. Journal what God showed you regarding placing all your trust in him.

Day 23

I don't really understand myself, for I want to do what is right, but I don't do it. Instead, I do what I hate. Romans 7:15 (NLT)

To grasp the message regarding sin, we must go back to the Garden of Eden, where man first fell from grace. Satan planted seeds of doubt when he questioned Eve whether she would surely die if she ate from the forbidden tree. Eve allowed herself to be deceived by Satan when he said her eyes would be opened, and then she would be as wise as God. The moment Adam and Eve ate the forbidden fruit, their eyes opened, and they realized their sin. Because of their rebellion to God, this opened the door to what we know as original sin.

Do you ever wake up and think today I am going to do things correctly? I will not let people frustrate me, or I will not have a bad attitude. Before you know it, you are ready to kill those around you and hide the bodies where they cannot be found! I think we can all relate to the frustrations that come with juggling a husband, children, work and chaotic schedules. That is when we have to stop and ask for forgiveness and ask God to change our attitude.

Paul did not deny the internal struggle between good and evil that lies within all of us. He wants us to understand that man cannot obey the law, because the law was incomplete until Christ was crucified and rose from the dead. After Christ's resurrection the Holy Spirit was sent so we can be overcomers. We must understand we only overcome our sinful nature if the Holy Spirit lives within us. We also must understand our mind is powerful, and the thoughts we allow will ultimately determine our actions. We must be careful about what we allow to enter our minds and guard our hearts so it

will not deceive us. To truly be with God, we must surrender our will and take our thoughts captive daily. The more time we spend in prayer, the more Christlike we become. To live a life consecrated to Him means laying our cares at the cross daily. Although we want to be obedient, our human nature allows us to deceive ourselves.

Prayer

Father, I struggle with my sinful nature. Help me not to become irritated when my life becomes chaotic. Please take my thoughts captive, so I may focus on you. Amen.

Read Romans 7: 13-16

Meditate on this passage of scripture as it highlights our own struggles in life. Journal your thoughts.

Day 24

To all who mourn in Israel, he will give a crown of beauty for ashes, a joyous blessing instead of mourning, festive praise instead of despair. In their righteousness, they will be like great oaks that the LORD has planted for his own glory. Isaiah 61:3 (NLT)

Ashes in Biblical times were representative of pain, loss, and even sin. People would often cover themselves in ashes, indicating they were in mourning. Oil was used for celebration when the bride's Father would anoint her with oil as a sign of consecration to the groom. We must appreciate that the book of Isaiah is representative of the coming Messiah, the bridegroom coming for His bride, and we are His bride! Even in the Old Testament, we can see the promise of Christ unfolding. Only Christ could trade beauty for ashes.

Think of your life as a book that only you and God can write. Just like a book, our life closes one chapter before we begin a new chapter. With each new chapter we learn, we grow, or we crash and burn. But the beautiful thing is God allows us to help write the chapters. We have free will to choose how each chapter unfolds. Through His grace, we can embrace what life throws at us or allow Satan to destroy us through resentment, anger, and negative self-talk. When tragedy comes our way, we can let God take that event and make something beautiful. When we devote our lives to Christ, each new chapter brings new blessings, and He turns our ashes to beauty. A life where we abide in Christ is a joyful life with Christ's anointing. How will your book be written?

Prayer

Father, I want to thank you for making something beautiful out of my mistakes. Help me to seek you first and make the right choices. Amen

Read Isaiah 61:3-5

Meditate on this passage of scripture. Journal about what God showed you during your time of meditation.

Day 25

I have been crucified with Christ and I no longer live, but Christ lives in me. The life I now live in the body, I live by faith in the Son of God, who loved me and gave himself for me. Galatians 2:20

This verse may be considered one of Paul's most significant proclamations. On the road to Damascus, Paul went through a radical transformation. However, some were still insistent that Christians should continue to uphold Jewish rules and were undermining Paul's authority. In his letter to the Galatians, Paul wants to establish that Jesus ultimately paid the price, and because of His sacrifice, they have been set free. He proclaims they are no longer justified by the works of the law but by our faith in Jesus Christ.

By the grace of God, we can become new creatures in Christ. When we invite Christ into our hearts, we are giving Him complete control. When we die to self-will and relinquish all control to Christ; we wholly surrender to His supremacy. It is imperative that we die to self daily and not allow sin to creep in. Living by faith is a journey, and as we grow closer to Christ, we are surrendering to God's will. When we abide in Christ, we allow Him to take up residence in our hearts. Through Christ, we have a new way of life where Christ's love replaces our sinful nature. Old ideas are dead, and we begin each day fresh! Hallelujah!

Prayer

Father, I have invited you into my life. Guide and direct me in my daily life, so I can surrender to your will. Amen.

Read Galatians 2: 20-21

Meditate on this passage of scripture. Journal what you think it means to be crucified with Christ.

Day 26

Then I heard the voice of the Lord saying, "Whom shall I send? And who will go for us? "And I said, "Here am I. Send me!" Isaiah 6:8

While in the presence of God, Isaiah was being called as a prophet to warn the people their wicked ways would destroy their land. Isaiah is awestruck with the vision God has given him. God needed someone with a willing heart to carry forth His message. The power of the Spirit of God was on Isaiah so firmly he could not hold the words back. The words flowed from his mouth; at that moment, he was willing to be utilized by God. These may very well be the most magnificent words Isaiah spoke. "Here am I; send me!"

We should aspire to have the Holy Spirit so strongly in our life that when we kneel in the presence of our Father, we feel the brush of angel's wings. The kind of relationship that consumes us to the very core of our being. We should hunger and thirst for more of our Savior.

To gain such inner strength that we will go wherever and do what he desires whatever the cost. This kind of transformation only comes when we are willing to be obedient and surrender our will to God. When we bring ourselves to a place where we freely and humbly submit to the purpose God created us for, he can use us. Let us all be willing to answer the call. May the spirit of the Lord be so intense in our life that we too will shout, "Here am I Lord, send me!"

Prayer

Father, I desire to have your Holy Spirit so dynamic in my life that I will be a willing servant and say "Here am I; send me." Let this be my prayer today.

Read Isaiah 6:8

Meditate on this passage of scripture. Think of a time God asked you to do something. Journal what it means to say "Here am I Lord, send me".

Day 27

The reason my Father loves me is that I lay down my life—only to take it up again. [18] No one takes it from me, but I lay it down of my own accord. I have authority to lay it down and authority to take it up again. This command I received from my Father." John 10:17-18

Jesus often used parables to illustrate His message in a way the disciples could understand. In this parable, it beautifully illustrates just how much a shepherd cares for his sheep. God then makes the comparison that He is a shepherd, and we are His sheep. This conveys to us that the true shepherd will go after the lost sheep.

To truly comprehend Jesus' message, we must first understand the deity of Jesus, fully man and fully God. He conveys that He willingly lays everything down for His children. However, Jesus wants us to know He had a choice. He establishes His divine authority to assert His will. Imagine if He had not chosen to let the cup pass, and had not said, "but not my will, but thy will be done."

What a magnificent example to demonstrate to us we have a wonderful gift called free will. We can lay our free will at the master's feet, or we can pick it up at any time. He will never force His will on us. How wonderful it is that we have a God that allows choice. Christ desires us to surrender all when we kneel in His presence. The option is ours; may we hunger and thirst to live a life fully surrendered to Him.

Prayer

Father, thank you for the beautiful gift of free will. Help me to make the right choices and surrender my will to bring you glory. Amen

Read John 10: 1-18

Meditate on this passage of scripture. Journal what God is saying to you about surrendering your will.

Day 28

Teach me to do your will, for you are my God; may your good Spirit lead me on level ground. Psalm 143:10

David was pleading for God's favor to manifest itself in his life. David was desperate to do God's will, yearning to walk in a way that would be pleasing to God. As we read the Psalms, we find David was a man after God's own heart.

Throughout scripture, God will speak to us if we allow Him to enter that sacred place in our hearts and minds. We must be willing to hear what God is saying to us. We can attain a place of deep yearning for God's favor if we will only be still and listen to God's voice. As the Psalmist says, "Cause me to hear thy loving kindness new each morning." If we are desperate for God's love to surround us, we will seek His will and embrace lessons from the Master. We must allow God to lead us to the garden where our soul will rest. In these quiet times, God will comfort us. He may draw us out of our comfort zone so we may grow. We work in the garden to get rid of the unnecessary weeds, which allows the flowers to flourish. God too will weed the sin from our soul and supply us with refreshing water so that we may flourish and become the person He created us to be.

God had a sovereign purpose for David's life from the time he was just a shepherd boy. He was handpicked and chosen by God with a divine purpose. Let us not forget we also were chosen; He knew us before we were born and designed us in His image.

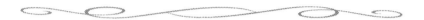

Prayer

Father, I desire to fulfill the purpose in which you designed me. Speak to me and show me the path that you want me to take. Help me to learn to walk in your will. Amen

Read Psalm 143

Meditate on this passage of scripture. Journal what it means to you to walk in God's will.

Day 29

Then the LORD said to Satan, "Have you considered my servant Job? There is no one on earth like him; he is blameless and upright, a man who fears God and shuns evil. Job 1:8

We cannot talk about obedience without mentioning Job. He was a devout man of God and lived a Holy life. God blessed Job with great wealth, Job 1:2-3 tells us he had seven sons, three daughters, owned three thousand sheep, three thousand camels, five hundred yoke of oxen, five hundred donkeys, and had a large number of servants.

Satan was searching for someone in which he could inflict mayhem. God asked Satan if he had considered his servant Job. God knew there was no one like him on earth for Job was righteous and faithful to God. God knew Job's faith was so strong that regardless of what Satan would do to him, he would never waiver in his faith. Satan wreaked havoc in Job's life, and Job remained faithful to God through it all.

Can we be thankful and remain faithful when trials come our way, or will Satan be able to consume us with grief, bitterness, and anxiety? Will we rise above the chaos in our world, with a historic pandemic, injustice, racism, and riots in the streets? Will we remain faithful if we lose a job, are financially ruined, or lose our precious child? We need to understand that God does not cause the devastation in our world today any more than He caused Job to suffer. God allowed Satan to test Job, and because He gave Satan dominion over the earth, bad things can happen to good people. We must also consider that God gave us the beautiful gift of free will; however, when we exercise free will, our choices have consequences, good or bad.

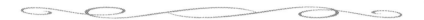

Prayer

Father, help me draw near to you during trial and teach me to have a Job kind of faith. Amen

Read Job 1:8

Meditate on this passage of scripture. Journal about a time when you needed a Job kind of faith.

Day 30

Father, if you are willing, remove this cup from me: yet not my will, but yours, be done. Luke 22:42

Luke describes Jesus' prayer in the garden, "his sweat was like drops of blood falling to the ground." It stands alone as the most influential account of a life surrendered. Jesus struggled in His humanness, asking to have the cup pass Him, but in his Godliness, He said, "not my will, but thy will be done." At this moment, Christ literally died to His human self. He paid the ultimate sacrifice when He said those words.

Throughout the Old Testament stories of men who were wholly devoted to God leap off the pages of the most excellent book ever written. Narratives unfold, revealing the promise of the coming Messiah.

Surrendering our will to him seems small, considering what Christ has given us. We can rest in the presence of God, and what a beautiful thing that is. Having this knowledge of the greatest story ever told, our life pales in comparison. His redeeming love is higher than anything we can imagine. The price he paid validates the depth of His love for us. God is the beginning and the end, the Alpha and Omega, the great I AM. We owe all to him! Reflecting on this scripture, I am drawn to the song "I Surrender All," written by Judson Van DeVenter. It was put to music by Winfield S. Weeden in 1896.

Prayer

Let this be our prayer today.

All to Jesus I Surrender, All to Him I freely give, I will ever love and trust him, In His presence daily live, I surrender all, I surrender all, all to thee my blessed savior, I surrender all. Amen.

Read Luke 22: 40-44

Meditate on this passage of scripture. Journal what it means to you personally, that Christ laid down His life for you.

Contemplate the words of the old hymn "Trust and Obey," written by John H. Sammis in 1887

"When we walk with the Lord in the light of his word,
what a glory he sheds on our way!

When we do his good will, he abodes with us still,
and with all who will trust and obey.
Trust and obey, for there's no other way
to be happy in Jesus, but to trust and obey."

"Trust and obey—for there's no other way
To be happy in Jesus, but to trust and obey."

What does this hymn mean to you?

Day 31

Do not conform to the pattern of this world, but be transformed by the renewing of your mind. Then you will be able to test and approve what God's will is—his good, pleasing and perfect will. Romans 12:2

Transformation is dramatic change in form or appearance. The most common example of transformation is the caterpillar changing into a beautiful butterfly. This transformation process occurs over a period of 10 days to several months. Spiritual transformation is a gradual process, it does not occur over night, and sometimes may take years to accomplish.

The first step in this transformation is awareness or need for change. When the caterpillar first hatches, he is very hungry and begins eating leaves until he is stuffed. He grows in diameter and in length, and then suddenly, signaled by hormones, he stops eating.

The caterpillar is destined for change and knows exactly when to stop eating. Humans transform spiritually at different times in our lives, and for different reasons. For some, it takes a horrible event to grab our attention, while others seem to have an easier route to transformation.

We as humans must acknowledge the need for change. Similar to the chapters in this devotion, transformation is the next step in the journey, after we have gone down the path of anxiety, bowed to Him in prayer, and hearing His voice we ultimately submit. It seems logical that transformation would come next. However, for some, it is harder than others, and perhaps it is in the obedience that we struggle. As we journey through the next ten days, prayerfully listen

for the voice of God, and submit your will and obey. The reward will be a transformed mind through Jesus Christ.

Prayer

Father we come to you to thank you for the things you are bringing to our attention. We know a change is needed within ourselves to become better human beings, so that your light will shine through us in a positive way. Amen

As you meditate on today's study, focus on where you want to be at the end of this study. What does your transformation look like?

Day 32

Therefore, if anyone is in Christ, the new creation has come:[a] The old has gone, the new is here!. 2 Corinthians 5:17

When the caterpillar stops eating, his body starts to die, and he starts eating himself. Enzymes are released that dissolves tissues, and some of the tissues and cells survive making the transformation to form a butterfly. To say it is a painful process is an understatement. Isn't our spiritual transformation painful? Habits are hard to break, and I am sure that many go back to old ways of thinking before their transformation is complete.

Zacchaeus, a rich tax collector, was transformed after one encounter with Jesus. After descending from the tree, he and Jesus went to his house for a meal. Although the Bible does not give a great amount of detail, Zacchaeus vowed to give half of his wealth to the poor and pay restitution for those he had cheated.

The name Simon Bar-Jones meant weak as sand, Jesus gave him a new life and a new name, Peter, which means strong as a rock.

Seeing a trend with the examples? Both changes and transformation occurred after an encounter with Jesus. Focus the next several days on your relationship with God, and in your quiet time, let Him do the talking and you listen. The Holy Spirit will speak to you and will lay things on your heart that you need to change. It is our responsibility to follow through to make those things happen.

Prayer

Father help us to seek your will in this transformation process, help us to be obedient in changing those things which you require of us. Your Son was perfect, may we strive to be more like him. Help us to understand that it is a daily process to make the necessary changes. Amen

Journal some of the ways your life has changed since Jesus became a part of your life.

Day 33

Forget the former things; do not dwell on the past. See, I am doing a new thing....... Isaiah 43:18-19

During our transformation, we work in partnership with the Holy Spirit to complete the process. Changes are required on our part, and as we obey and complete the necessary steps, we are drawn closer and His voice becomes clearer. This transformation is part of sanctification where our souls are purified. We are created in the image of Christ, for He has given us talents and gifts for He does not want to see us struggle. Positive self-talk is essential for us to move to the next level, we are overcomers thru Christ.

What are you struggling with? Is addiction a part of your life, or do you struggle with memories of abuse? Let go of the thoughts and pray for release from the addiction. Seek help, get counseling. Decide today that you are not who they say you are, you are who He says you are. You are a child of the King, created in His likeness and for His glory. Transformation of your thoughts are key to living a transformed life. You are in control of the thoughts you allow in your head! We cannot continue to believe the lies in our head when Jesus Christ is now our landlord. Satan and his lies are not paying rent, only taking up space! Kick him out today and let the healing and transformation begin,

Meditate on God's word, listen to Christian music, watch wholesome shows, and be around positive people! What goes in your mind will come out of your mouth and be reflected in your actions and the way you treat others.

Prayer

Father I pray that you help me to renew my mind and live a life that is pleasing to you. Help me to disregard old memories forever, that I may move forward in my walk with you. Transform me Lord so that I may be more like you. Amen

During your quiet time, journal some of the things you must learn to overcome.

Day 34

But the fruit of the Spirit is love, joy, peace, forbearance, kindness, goodness, faithfulness, gentleness and self-control. Against such things there is no law. Galatians 5:22-23

How will we know when we "have arrived" and are fully transformed? Transformation is a process and we will never be completely transformed. Jesus was perfect, and unfortunately, we are not and never will be. We will always be striving for perfection.

Can we gauge our progress towards transformation? Certainly, we can. We bear "fruit" when we are living a transformed life. Many of these fruitful qualities are listed in Galatians, chapter 5. These are living proof that Christ is living in us.

Transformation is like the pruning a vinedresser performs on the branches. Sometimes the branches are cut way back so that the fruit will begin producing again. Transformation requires us to take away certain things in our life. "Every branch in me that beareth not fruit he taketh away". John 15:2 (KJC)

In Bruce Wilkinson's book, *Secrets of the Vine*, pruning is compared to discipline. Our Father may need to prune or take something away from us because we are not being fruitful or obedient.

Are you bearing the right kind of fruit? If you wish to continue the path towards transformation, you will need to address any short comings.

Prayer

Father open our eyes and reveal the fruit that we are producing, help us to mirror the qualities of the fruit of the spirit. Prune us when necessary and guide us as we strive to be more like you. Amen

In your quiet time, journal about the times you may have been through a pruning process.

Day 35

It is for freedom that Christ has set us free. Stand firm, then, and do not let yourselves be burdened again by a yoke of slavery. Galatians 5:1

Bondage is the state of being a slave. Bondage can come in many forms; financial, spiritual, and relational. Spiritual bondage is anything that is prohibiting us from being fully submitted to the Holy Spirit's direction and presence in our lives.

According to Wikipedia, slavery is a Greek verb *skyleuo*, which means "to strip a slain enemy". Prior to the Civil War, the slaves were stripped of their freedom, their property and many times they were stripped of their families. The slaves were property of the new owners and had no rights. Rules were many, and they were beaten if they disobeyed. They did as they were told, and their lives were ruled by one master, the plantation owner.

If we allow Satan to rule our thoughts and minds, spiritual bondage occurs. In the gospel of Matthew, we are told we cannot serve two masters. When God created Adam and Eve, they were given a free will. Using this free will, they made a wrong choice, which has affected us now for generations. You can make the change and choose the right path for your life. Once the choice is made, you will be released from the bondage that once held you. I want to caution you, once you are released from bondage, this does not mean you can never be a slave again. You must die to self daily.

Prayer

Father help me to break free from the bondage of sin and my past. Forgive me where I have failed to walk with you daily. Bring things to my mind that need to be removed from my life. Just a closer walk with you is my desire. Amen

As you pray today, focus on the things that are holding you bondage, asking for release.

Day 36

For I know the plans I have for you, declares the Lord, plans to prosper you and not to harm you, plans to give you hope and a future. Jeremiah 29:11 (NIV)

Transformation can be painful. But scripture tells us that the Lord knows the plans for us, plans not to harm us and give us hope.

Several things will occur when you are in the process of transformation. The Holy Spirit may bring people to our attention that may be a bad influence on our life. The removal of people in your life can be very painful. Examine their behavior and ask yourself, are they displaying the fruits of the spirit? Remember, we are moving forward to a new life and must leave the old behind.

In an earlier devotion, we talked about the things that we allow to enter in our mind, will come out our mouth or show up in our transformation actions? The same thing goes for memories of the past. If we do not forgive and let things go, we will repeat the treatment we received. Naaman was told to dip in the muddy waters of the Jordan River seven times to receive his full healing. This is an example of leaving the old behind and accepting the new life. He was obedient and dipped seven times. I am sure he questioned Elisha's command and probably thought he was a little crazy to have him dip in a muddy river for healing. We may have to go through some things during our transformation may be confusing, but we must remember, our God is sovereign and knows the future.

Prayer

Father be with me during this time, guide and direct my paths. Bring to light the things you want me to change. Help me trust in you during this process, knowing that you will be gentle in the pruning process. Amen

Write in your journal today things that you have let go in the past, and how your life is better now.

Day 37

And the God of all grace, who called you to his eternal glory in Christ, after you have suffered a little while, will himself restore you and make you strong, firm and steadfast. 1 Peter 5:10

While pain is the physical experience, suffering is an emotional experience. The Bible has several examples of suffering during one's life transformation. Priscilla and Aquila were forced to leave their home in Rome, everything they knew was taken from them. Leaving Rome, they would have left friends behind as well as the tent making business which provided a living for them.

This suffering or emotional pain they felt during this time was preparing them for God's plan for their life. God used their suffering to mold them into the Christian leaders and prepare them for the work they would be doing with Paul in the early church in Corinth.

King David was an example of a great man of God, but he was not without failure or hardships. David was destined as leader from an early age after the fall of King Saul. At God's direction, Samuel went to Bethlehem to the house of Jesse and asked to see his sons. After all the sons were presented and rejected by Samuel, David was ultimately chosen and anointed by Samuel to be the next King.

King David's journey as king was a tumultuous one, and many times he failed God. He lusted after Bathsheba, impregnated her and sent her husband into a battle where he was killed. This story is not what you would expect of a King chosen by God. David was called a man after God's own heart. Although he sinned, he was remorseful and sought council with the Lord.

Our journey will be much like David's, peaks and valleys along the way. We must make the decision to stay the course.

Prayer

Father forgive me where I have failed you in my journey. Help me to make better choices and to understand the consequences that may come my way. Amen

Meditate on the things that you have experienced in the valley, and journal about those experiences and what you learned.

Let us not become weary in doing good, for at the proper time we will reap a harvest if we do not give up" Galatians 6:9 (NIV)

In Corinthians, Paul writes about the race that we are to run with endurance. One could compare transformation to a race, just as training for a marathon can be compared to the Christian life and road to transformation.

On a road to transformation, a novice runner would seek advice, and we too must take advice from wise counsel. These individuals can help keep us on the right path and be an accountability partner.

During this process we should develop a training routine or daily Bible study. Set aside a certain time of day, if possible, and make your study of the word a priority.

Appropriate gear for a runner is key to a safe and successful run. A Bible and several study guides for the new Christian are the required basics. As you grow stronger in your faith, Bible commentaries are good for in-depth research.

Mental preparation for a runner is especially important, and as a Christian we must not get discouraged during setbacks, focus on the prize and keep moving forward. You must visualize a successful outcome, always focus on what lies ahead, not what is behind you.

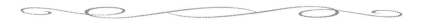

Prayer

Father help me to focus daily on you and not let distractions get in my way. Strengthen me and show me your ways, forgive me where I fail you. Help me to focus on the prize. Amen

Are you prepared for the journey? If not, what do you need to prepare to get ready? Journal your thoughts

Day 39

..........Let us run with patience the race set before us.
Hebrews 12:1

As we run this race of transformation and living the Christian life, it will be difficult, and we will want to give up and quit. We have already decided by accepting Christ as our Savior that this is the race for us. Let Christ guide you as we continue the race.

As with any race there will be obstacles and set- backs. You may need to adjust your stride and slow down a little bit. The key will be to stay in the race and do not throw in the towel. Revelations chapter 2:10 tells us, "Do not be afraid of what you are about to suffer". This verse is clear that we will have troubles in this world and on our journey.

When we have trials that are threatening our journey, we must stay on course and remain faithful. God tells us that we will receive the crown of life at the end. We will receive everything He has promised if we do not give up or listen to the other voices that try to distract us daily. Keep yourself isolated from unbelief; stay positive and stay in the Word.

In his letter to Timothy, Paul is mentoring him and showing him things that need to be done. He knew his time on earth was short, and he wrote in this letter, "I have fought the good fight. I have finished the race. I have kept the faith".

Paul's letter tells us this race is a battle, we must have faith, and continue to fight until the end.

Prayer

Father give me strength to endure trials that may come my way today. Help me to focus on you and the race before me. Amen

During your quiet time, talk to the Holy Spirit about those things that make you tired. Journal about your time with him today.

Day 40

Being confident of this, that he who began a good work in you will carry it on to completion until the day of Christ Jesus. Philippians 1:6

As we have realized, transformation is a journey, but we know that if we bear the fruit of the Spirit we are progressing. Here are some ways to help you to transform your life:

It is essential that we spend time daily in prayer and in God's word. Working towards an intimate relationship with Him requires us to communicate with Him daily. If we are communicating daily, then we will hear the Holy Spirit speak to us. As we encounter the Holy Spirit, we must be willing to obey His commands and follow His leading. We must trust the Holy Spirit will guide and direct us in our daily lives.

Our lives need to reflect the holiness of the Father. Our actions and our words need to match what we are professing in our lives. Our beliefs are to be shared with others and to teach the lost and hurting about the love of Jesus Christ.

Trusting God with the details of our lives is a way for us to surrender control. He must have a willing vessel for us to live a transformed life. We must be in-tune to the voice of the Holy Spirit and be willing to make the necessary changes.

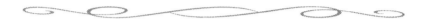

Prayer

Father quiet our heart and our minds today so the Holy Spirit can speak to us. Let us purify our vessels and present them to you to be refilled. Amen

As you write in your journal today, be honest with yourself, are you spending quality time with the Lord, or is prayer an afterthought?

CALMING THE STORM
STUDY GUIDE

The issue of fear is so important that scripture references it more than 300 times. Let us take a closer look at how the Bible tells us to cope with anxiety. We must cling to this promise daily if we are to overcome fear. God does not want us to be exhausted to the point that we lose hope. If you are feeling depressed or are struggling to get through a trial in your life, remember to lean on your Father and remember His promises.

In the Psalm below, God divinely shows us how very much we are valued.

[13] For you created my inmost being; you knit me together in my mother's womb.[14] I praise you because I am fearfully and wonderfully made; your works are wonderful, I know that full well.[15] My frame was not hidden from you when I was made in the secret place, when I was woven together in the depths of the earth.[16] Your eyes saw my unformed body; all the days ordained for me were written in your book before one of them came to be. Psalm 139:13-16 (NIV)

Think of a time in your life that you did not feel you were valued?

How did you cope with it or did you bury it deep within?

⁷ Cast all your anxiety on him because he cares for you.⁸ Be alert and of sober mind. Your enemy the devil prowls around like a roaring lion looking for someone to devour. ⁹ Resist him, standing firm in the faith, because you know that the family of believers throughout the world is undergoing the same kind of sufferings.¹⁰ And the God of all grace, who called you to his eternal glory in Christ, after you have suffered a little while, will himself restore you and make you strong, firm and steadfast. 1 Peter 5:7-10

Think of a time when you were so overwhelmed with anxiety that you found it difficult to trust. What steps did you take to overcome the anxiety so you could function?

Peter reminds us that this world is Satan's domain and he will stop at nothing to annihilate our life.

Describe a time when Satan sought to destroy your life.

Nay the God of hope fill you with all joy and peace as you trust in him, so that you may overflow with hope by the power of the Holy Spirit. Romans 15:13

What have you found most helpful in keeping hope alive in your life?

Cast your cares on the LORD and he will sustain you; he will never let the righteous; be shaken. Psalm 55:22

After reading the above scripture, describe how you cast your cares upon the Lord.

For everything that was written in the past was written to teach us, so that through the endurance taught in the Scriptures and the encouragement they provide we might have hope. Romans 15:4

Why it is important to hide scripture in our hearts?

From the ends of the earth I call to you, I call as my heart grows faint; lead me to the rock that is higher than I. Psalm 61:2

What is the rock David is referring to in this scripture?

For further reflection read Psalm 91. Journal below what God is speaking to you through this Psalm.

Peace I leave with you, my peace I give unto you: not as the world giveth, give I unto you. Let not your heart be troubled, neither let it be afraid. John 14:27

Read John 14. Envision you are there, and Jesus is saying this directly to you. How does it make you feel?

Further reading:

John 14:27
Galatians 6:9
Psalm 91

ATTITUDE OF PRAYER
STUDY GUIDE

Definition of Prayer: A solemn request for help or expression of thanks addressed to God; a set order of words used in praying; the act or practice of praying to God kneeling in prayer.

Prayer time is an important part of our journey on the road to transformation. It is a two- way communication with the Father, and our prayer time is where the Holy Spirit speaks to us and guides us. The Holy Spirit gives us wisdom, understanding, discernment and is our comforter. Coming to the Father in prayer requires several things of us. In 1 Thessalonians 5: 17, he tells us to pray without ceasing. As we proceed into the study, the requirements of our prayer time are outlined for you. I recommend that you read the scriptures so that you can fully understand what God wants from us during the intimate time with him.

Our first step in prayer is coming to the Father with the right attitude. What does Mark 11:24, and Matthew 6:6 instruct us to do to prepare for prayer?

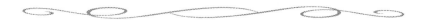

Why do you think it is important to have an attitude of prayer?

When we pray often, we are praying for our own needs. Read for following scripture for further guidance on who to pray for, Job 42:10, Luke 6:27-28. Who are we to pray for?

Is it hard for you to pray for others? Especially those that have wronged you.

What does God tell us that we should pray for? Philippians 4:6, James 5:14-16

What does scripture say we must do for our prayers to be answered? Mark 11:24, 25

Do you think faith is important for you to have when you pray? Why?

When we prayer the Lord responds in various ways. Read Jer. 29:12, Acts 2:21 Job 22:27 and 42:10,

Why do you think prayers go unanswered?

How did prayer help Jesus in Matt. Chapter 4 when he was led into the wilderness by the Holy Spirit to fast and pray?

Do you think Jesus' recent baptism had anything to do with Satan tempting him? Discuss how this applies to your life.

More scriptures to read on elements of sincere prayer:

Matt. 6:9-10 1 John 1:9 1 Timothy 2:1-3 James 5:15 Phil. 4:6

SURRENDERING TO GOD'S WILL STUDY GUIDE

If we as Christians do not experience or know how deep God's love for us is, then we cannot begin to fathom what Paul is describing in the scripture below. This passage of scripture is the essence of the deep relationship we should all desire to have with our Heavenly Father.

For this reason I kneel before the Father, [15] from whom every family[a] in heaven and on earth derives its name. [16] I pray that out of his glorious riches he may strengthen you with power through his Spirit in your inner being, [17] so that Christ may dwell in your hearts through faith. And I pray that you, being rooted and established in love, [18] may have power, together with all the Lord's holy people, to grasp how wide and long and high and deep is the love of Christ, [19] and to know this love that surpasses knowledge—that you may be filled to the measure of all the fullness of God. Now to him who is able to do immeasurably more than all we ask or imagine, according to his power that is at work within us, Ephesians 3: 14-20

While contemplating on this scripture describe what gives you the most peace.

Describe a time in your life when the fullness of God became real to you.

but now revealed and made known through the prophetic writings by the command of the eternal God, so that all the Gentiles might come to the obedience that comes from[a] faith—Romans 16:26

What do you think it means when Paul states it is made manifest by the scriptures of the prophets?

Do you not know that your bodies are temples of the Holy Spirit, who is in you, whom you have received from God? You are not your own; [20] you were bought at a price. Therefore, honor God with your bodies. 1 Corinthians 6:19-20

What does Paul mean when he tells the church at Corinth their body is the temple of the Holy Ghost?

What does it mean to glorify God in our body, and our spirit?

Then he said to them all: "Whoever wants to be my disciple must deny themselves and take up their cross daily and follow me. [24] For whoever wants to save their life will lose it, but whoever loses their life for me will save it. Luke 9:23-24

What does it mean to pick up our cross daily?

Think of a time in your life when it was difficult to pick up your cross. How did you deal with the situation? Was your resolve in dealing with that situation pleasing to God?

In your relationships with one another, have the same mindset as Christ Jesus:

⁶ Who, being in very nature[,] God did not consider equality with God something to be used to his own advantage; rather, he made himself nothing by taking the very nature[b] of a servant, being made in human likeness. And being found in appearance as a man, he humbled himself by becoming obedient to death even death on a cross. Philippians 2:5-8

What significance does this mean to you to be a coheir with Christ?

What responsibility does this connection give to you?

if my people, who are called by **my** name, will humble themselves and pray and seek **my** face and turn from their wicked ways, then I will hear from heaven, and I will forgive their sin and will heal their land. 2 Chronicles 7:14

With this scripture in mind, how would you construct your prayer regarding controversial issues such as racism, sexuality, and immorality?

ROAD TO A TRANSFORMED LIFE STUDY GUIDE

We have been on this transformation journey for 40 days now. In the Old Testament, the number 40 is significant and referred to in several books. Spies were sent by Moses to explore the land of Canaan and were gone 40 days, the Hebrew people wandered for 40 years outside the promised land, and in the book of Numbers, it says it takes 40 years for a new generation to arise.

While in the New Testament, the gospels report that Jesus was in the wilderness for 40 days after being baptized by John the Baptist. In this account, he was led into the wilderness by the Holy Spirit for prayer and fasting. The devil tried to tempt him without success. Our road to transformation is like being in the wilderness, the devil will tempt us as we grow closer to God.

The goal in transformation is to be like Christ. What does Galatians 4:19 tell us about transformation?

Do you think you were predestined to be like Christ? What does Romans 8:29 tell you?

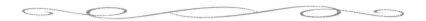

What does 2 Corinthians 5:17 and Galatians 2:20 tell you about the old and the new?

Service to God is an example of a transformed life. What instructions does Romans 12:3-8 give us?

What is another trait of a transformed life? Romans 12:10

As we mentioned this is a journey and does not occur overnight. What does Romans 12: 11-12 tell us about this?

True transformation requires faith. Faith allows us to see past our current state and trust God for the future. What does Hebrews 11:6 tell us about faith?

AFTERWARD

The authors were childhood friends and had experienced many life events together. They had talked many times about writing a devotion, and both had kept journals of their thoughts throughout the years. They used these journals as the basis of the devotion which was written during COVID 19 2020.

The world, as we know, it ceased to exist. Due to the Pandemic, the world shut down. Fear ravaged our world as businesses closed, millions were unemployed overnight, and leaders advised us to shelter at home.

The devastation wreaked havoc in European cities, New York City, and many other metropolitan cities across the US. Hospitals were overwhelmed with triaging the vast number of patients flooding into Emergency departments. We watched in terror as stadiums were transformed into hospitals. Refrigerated trucks were turned into morgues. Navy hospital ships were taken to New York harbor and California to assist with massive patient overload.

Our generation had never experienced a pandemic such as this. As we lived in isolation separated from families and friends, we eventually found a new normal. We left our homes only for essential items such as medication and groceries. We were advised to wear masks and social distance at least 6 feet when in public. We prayed

for normal again as we learned to have church and Sunday school online or virtually. However, we vowed to learn and not take for granted the freedoms we are blessed with.

During the COVID 19 pandemic there was an incident of police brutality where a black man was killed and witnessed by many. This incident sparked racial conflict which triggered protests, some of which became riots. Many of the riots became violent with even more bloodshed. Rioters overtook police stations, city halls, blocked freeways, destroyed businesses and historical monuments We found ourselves a nation at war with itself.

BIBLIOGRAPHY

1. **Process of How** Trees Absorb and Evaporate Water

    www.thoughtco.com/process-of-using-water-by-trees-1343505

2. Knight, George W; Ray, Rayburn W. The Illustrated Everyday Bible Companion 2005, Barbour, New York p.272

3. Wikipedia, retrieved 5/26/2020

4. Wilkinson, Bruce. Secrets of the Vine. 2001. Multmomah Publishers, Inc. Sisters OR

5. New International Version (NIV) utilized unless otherwise indicated.

6. King James Version (KJV)

7. New Living Translation (NLT)

ABOUT THE AUTHORS

Donna and Sheila have been lifelong friends and are co-founders of Beautifully Woven Ministries which started as a private Facebook group where women could encourage and support each other by posting prayer requests and scripture. Through their trials in life, they feel God has prepared them for this journey in writing this devotion and starting the ministry.

Sheila Vanaman, born and raised in Oklahoma, currently resides in Owasso with her husband, John. They have a blended family which includes 2 sons, one of which is deceased and 2 daughters. The Vanaman's have 7 grandchildren, and 2 great grandchildren. Sheila holds a bachelor's degree in Nursing from Oklahoma City University, beginning her career in 1993 with an Associates Degree in Nursing from Rogers State College. She holds certificates from Light University in Christian Life Coaching for Women and Christian Counseling for Ministry. She attends Christ United Methodist Church in Tulsa, where they are actively involved with the Two-by-Two Sunday School Class, which they co-founded with Pastor Jim and Barbara Stillwell in 2003. Sheila has worked with Pastor Jim to plan and facilitate multiple groups retreats.

Donna Hopkins Smith is a life long Oklahoman. She met her husband Tracy in high school and have been married for 43 years. They have 2 children, Brandy and Matthew and 6 grandsons. She

is a Registered Nurse, beginning her career in 1989 as an Associate Degree Nurse graduating from Northern Oklahoma College, and holds a Master's in Nursing from the University of Oklahoma. She also is a Certified Clinical Nurse Leader, one of the first in the state of Oklahoma. Donna attends Extreme Church in Pryor, OK where she is involved with the Women's Ministry, facilitates Life Groups, and is responsible for social media posts.

Journal

Journal

_____
_____
_____
_____
_____
_____
_____
_____
_____
_____
_____
_____
_____
_____
_____
_____
_____
_____
_____
_____
_____
_____
_____
_____
_____
_____
_____
_____
_____
_____
_____

Journal

_____
_____
_____
_____
_____
_____
_____
_____
_____
_____
_____
_____
_____
_____
_____
_____
_____
_____
_____
_____
_____
_____
_____
_____
_____
_____
_____
_____
_____
_____
_____
_____

Journal

Journal

_____
_____
_____
_____
_____
_____
_____
_____
_____
_____
_____
_____
_____
_____
_____
_____
_____
_____
_____
_____
_____
_____
_____
_____
_____
_____
_____
_____
_____
_____

Journal

Journal

_____
_____
_____
_____
_____
_____
_____
_____
_____
_____
_____
_____
_____
_____
_____
_____
_____
_____
_____
_____
_____
_____
_____
_____
_____
_____
_____
_____
_____
_____

Journal

Journal

Journal

Journal

_____
_____
_____
_____
_____
_____
_____
_____
_____
_____
_____
_____
_____
_____
_____
_____
_____
_____
_____
_____
_____
_____
_____
_____
_____
_____
_____

Journal

Journal

_____
_____
_____
_____
_____
_____
_____
_____
_____
_____
_____
_____
_____
_____
_____
_____
_____
_____
_____
_____
_____
_____
_____
_____
_____
_____
_____
_____
_____
_____
_____
_____

Journal

Journal

_____
_____
_____
_____
_____
_____
_____
_____
_____
_____
_____
_____
_____
_____
_____
_____
_____
_____
_____
_____
_____
_____
_____
_____
_____
_____
_____
_____
_____

Journal

_____
_____
_____
_____
_____
_____
_____
_____
_____
_____
_____
_____
_____
_____
_____
_____
_____
_____
_____
_____
_____
_____
_____
_____
_____
_____
_____
_____
_____
_____

Journal

_____
_____
_____
_____
_____
_____
_____
_____
_____
_____
_____
_____
_____
_____
_____
_____
_____
_____
_____
_____
_____
_____
_____
_____
_____
_____
_____
_____
_____
_____
_____
_____

Journal

_____
_____
_____
_____
_____
_____
_____
_____
_____
_____
_____
_____
_____
_____
_____
_____
_____
_____
_____
_____
_____
_____
_____
_____
_____
_____
_____
_____
_____
_____

Journal

_____
_____
_____
_____
_____
_____
_____
_____
_____
_____
_____
_____
_____
_____
_____
_____
_____
_____
_____
_____
_____
_____
_____
_____
_____
_____
_____
_____
_____

Journal

Journal

_____
_____
_____
_____
_____
_____
_____
_____
_____
_____
_____
_____
_____
_____
_____
_____
_____
_____
_____
_____
_____
_____
_____
_____
_____
_____
_____
_____
_____
_____
_____
_____
_____
_____

Journal

SHEILA VANAMAN; DONNA HOPKINS SMITH

Journal

Journal

Journal

_____
_____
_____
_____
_____
_____
_____
_____
_____
_____
_____
_____
_____
_____
_____
_____
_____
_____
_____
_____
_____
_____
_____
_____
_____
_____
_____
_____
_____
_____
_____
_____

Journal

Journal

_____

_____

_____

_____

_____

_____

_____

_____

_____

_____

_____

_____

_____

_____

_____

_____

_____

_____

_____

_____

_____

_____

_____

_____

_____

_____

_____

_____

_____

_____

Journal

Journal

_____
_____
_____
_____
_____
_____
_____
_____
_____
_____
_____
_____
_____
_____
_____
_____
_____
_____
_____
_____
_____
_____
_____
_____
_____
_____
_____

Journal

_____
_____
_____
_____
_____
_____
_____
_____
_____
_____
_____
_____
_____
_____
_____
_____
_____
_____
_____
_____
_____
_____
_____
_____
_____
_____
_____
_____
_____
_____
_____
_____
_____

Journal

Journal

Journal

Journal

Journal

_____
_____
_____
_____
_____
_____
_____
_____
_____
_____
_____
_____
_____
_____
_____
_____
_____
_____
_____
_____
_____
_____
_____
_____
_____
_____
_____
_____
_____

Journal

Journal

_____
_____
_____
_____
_____
_____
_____
_____
_____
_____
_____
_____
_____
_____
_____
_____
_____
_____
_____
_____
_____
_____
_____
_____
_____
_____
_____
_____
_____
_____
_____
_____
_____

Journal

_____
_____
_____
_____
_____
_____
_____
_____
_____
_____
_____
_____
_____
_____
_____
_____
_____
_____
_____
_____
_____
_____
_____
_____
_____
_____
_____
_____
_____
_____
_____

Journal

_____
_____
_____
_____
_____
_____
_____
_____
_____
_____
_____
_____
_____
_____
_____
_____
_____
_____
_____
_____
_____
_____
_____
_____
_____
_____
_____
_____
_____
_____

Journal

Journal

_____
_____
_____
_____
_____
_____
_____
_____
_____
_____
_____
_____
_____
_____
_____
_____
_____
_____
_____
_____
_____
_____
_____
_____
_____
_____
_____
_____
_____
_____
_____
_____

Journal

Journal

_____
_____
_____
_____
_____
_____
_____
_____
_____
_____
_____
_____
_____
_____
_____
_____
_____
_____
_____
_____
_____
_____
_____
_____
_____
_____
_____
_____
_____
_____

Journal

Journal

_____
_____
_____
_____
_____
_____
_____
_____
_____
_____
_____
_____
_____
_____
_____
_____
_____
_____
_____
_____
_____
_____
_____
_____
_____
_____
_____
_____
_____
_____
_____
_____
_____

Journal

_____
_____
_____
_____
_____
_____
_____
_____
_____
_____
_____
_____
_____
_____
_____
_____
_____
_____
_____
_____
_____
_____
_____
_____
_____
_____
_____
_____
_____
_____
_____

Journal

_____
_____
_____
_____
_____
_____
_____
_____
_____
_____
_____
_____
_____
_____
_____
_____
_____
_____
_____
_____
_____
_____
_____
_____
_____
_____
_____
_____
_____
_____
_____

Journal

Journal

_____
_____
_____
_____
_____
_____
_____
_____
_____
_____
_____
_____
_____
_____
_____
_____
_____
_____
_____
_____
_____
_____
_____
_____
_____
_____
_____
_____
_____
_____
_____
_____

Journal

Printed in the United States
By Bookmasters